Let's Eat

Foods of Our World

by Janine Scott

Content and Reading Adviser: Mary Beth Fletcher, Ed.D.
Educational Consultant/Reading Specialist
The Carroll School, Lincoln, Massachusetts

Spyglass
BOOKS

COMPASS POINT BOOKS

Minneapolis, Minnesota

Compass Point Books
3722 West 50th Street, #115
Minneapolis, MN 55410

Visit Compass Point Books on the Internet at *www.compasspointbooks.com*
or e-mail your request to *custserv@compasspointbooks.com*

Project Manager: Rebecca Weber McEwen
Editor: Heidi Schoof
Photo Researcher: Image Select International Limited
Photo Selectors: Rebecca Weber McEwen and Heidi Schoof
Designers: Les Tranby and Jaime Martens

Library of Congress Cataloging-in-Publication Data

Scott, Janine.
  Let's eat : foods of our world / by Janine Scott.
      p. cm. — (Spyglass books)
Includes bibliographical references and index.
  ISBN 0-7565-0365-5 (hardcover)
  1. Food—Juvenile literature. 2. Food habits—Juvenile literature.
[1. Food. 2. Food habits.] I. Title. II. Series.
  TX355 .S35 2002
  641.3—dc21

                                    2002002560

Contents

Taste of the World 4

Hot and Spicy 6

Nutty About Nuts 8

Nice Rice 10

Cereal for Dinner? 12

Eat Your Greens 14

Milk It! 16

Meaty Morsels 18

Sugary Sweet 20

Glossary 22

Learn More 23

Index 24

Taste of the World

People who live in different places eat different things. This is because a country can only grow food that suits its *climate* or its weather.

Extra Helping
People in different countries may eat the same food, but cook it in different ways.

Hot and Spicy

Wow! That's hot! In many countries, people use spices such as **chili powder** to make food hot and spicy.

Spices usually come from plants that grow in hot places.

Extra Helping
Curry powder is popular in Asia and India.

Nutty About Nuts

Nuts are used in cooking all around the world. Some nuts are dried. Some are eaten raw. Other nuts need to be cooked.

Extra Helping
Coconuts grow on palm trees. Palm trees grow in hot places such as this tropical *island.*

Peanuts

Nice Rice

Rice is an important food. It helps to feed more than half the people in the world.

Rice can be ground into rice flour and made into bread.

Extra Helping
Rice grows well in warm, wet places, such as China and Japan.

Cereal for Dinner?

Grains, or cereals, include oats, rye, corn, rice, and wheat.

Noodles and pasta are made from grains, too.

Extra Helping
Breakfast cereals and breads are usually made from grains.

Eat Your Greens

Vegetables and fruits come in all shapes and sizes.

Some grow well in wet, hot countries. Others need cooler climates.

Extra Helping
The potato is a *root* vegetable popular in many countries.

Watermelon

Milk It!

Milk comes from animals such as cows, goats, and sheep. It can be turned into cheese, butter, cream, ice cream, and yogurt.

Extra Helping
In many places, animals are still milked by hand.

Meaty Morsels

Meat and fish are part of many people's diets.

Fresh fish markets let people eat fish that may have been caught on the other side of the world that same day.

Extra Helping
Seafood is a big
part of the
Japanese diet.
It is often
eaten raw.

19

Sugary Sweet

Most of the world's sugar comes from sugar cane and sugar beets.

Some people sweeten their food with honey.

Extra Helping

The *sap* from sugar maple trees drips into buckets. It is then made into maple syrup.

21

Glossary

chili powder–a spice made from dried chili peppers

climate–the way the weather usually is in a certain area, such as hot or rainy

curry powder–a mixture of spices

island–an area of land surrounded by water

root–the part of a plant that grows underground

sap–the liquid inside of a plant

Learn More

Books

Suhr, Mandy. *When I Eat.* Minneapolis, Minn.: Carolrhoda Books, 1992.

Thomson, Ruth. *Grandma's Garden.* Illustrated by Evie Safarewicz. New York: DK Publishing, 1999.

Web Sites

www.brainpop.com
(click on "Nutrition")

www.cookalotamus.com

www.nutritionexplorations.org/ kids_zone.html

Index

bread, 10, 12
cheese, 16
coconut, 8
fish, 18
pasta, 12

peanuts, 9
rice, 10
spices, 6
sugar cane, 20
syrup, 21

GR: H
Word Count: 215

From Janine Scott

I live in New Zealand, and have two daughters. They love to read books that are full of fun facts and features. I hope you do, too!